Space
Sticker
Book

Illustrated by Paul Nicholls

Designed by Non Taylor

Written by Fiona Watt

Space consultant: Stuart Atkinson

Contents

What's out in Space?

Looking up into the sky on a clear night, it's possible to see over 3,000 twinkling stars. If you look through a telescope you might see even more amazing things, such as planets, satellites, comets and meteor showers.

Fill the pages with stickers of things these sky watchers might see.

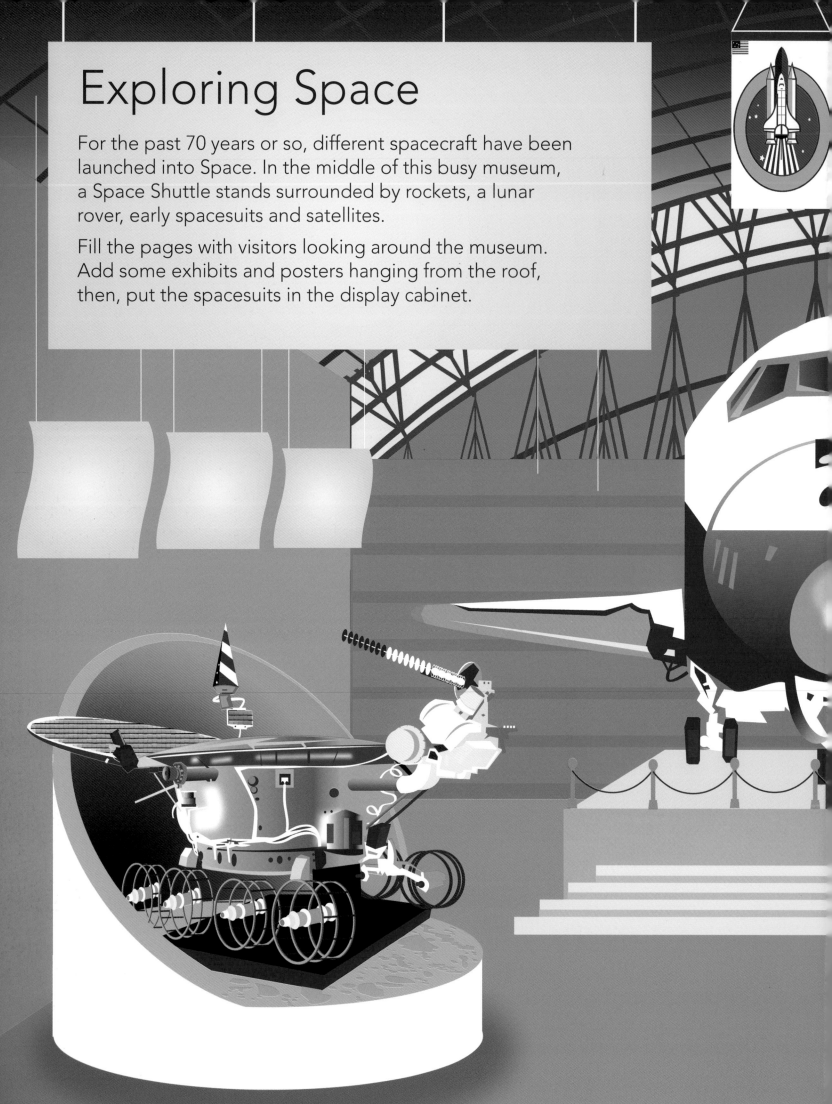

Exploring Space

For the past 70 years or so, different spacecraft have been launched into Space. In the middle of this busy museum, a Space Shuttle stands surrounded by rockets, a lunar rover, early spacesuits and satellites.

Fill the pages with visitors looking around the museum. Add some exhibits and posters hanging from the roof, then, put the spacesuits in the display cabinet.

COMMAND
MODULE

SERVICE
MODULE

Experimental
pressure suit
1968

EX-1A suit
1967

Glenn
1962

Gagarin
1961

The first men on the Moon

It's 20th July 1969. Millions of people around the world are glued to their televisions as Neil Armstrong and then Buzz Aldrin, take the first steps on the Moon.

Press on the stickers of the astronauts, their footprints and the scientific equipment they will use while they are there.

Meet some astronauts

It's been over 50 years since the first person flew into Space. These two modern astronauts are being helped into spacesuits that they will wear while taking off and landing, and during a spacewalk.

Use the stickers to dress the astronauts.

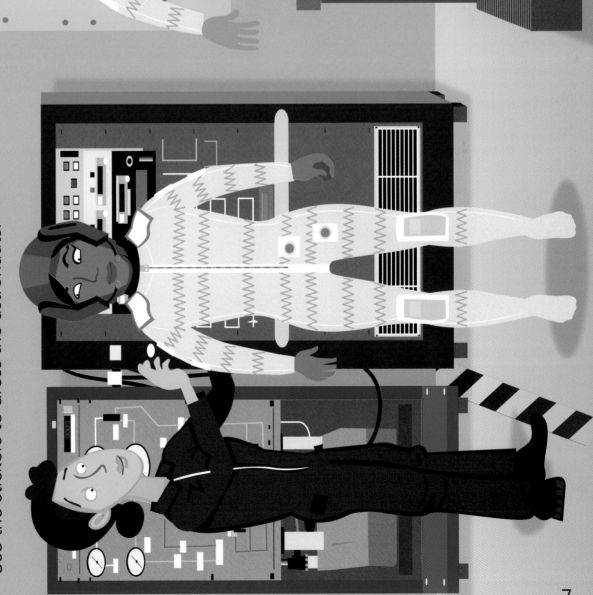

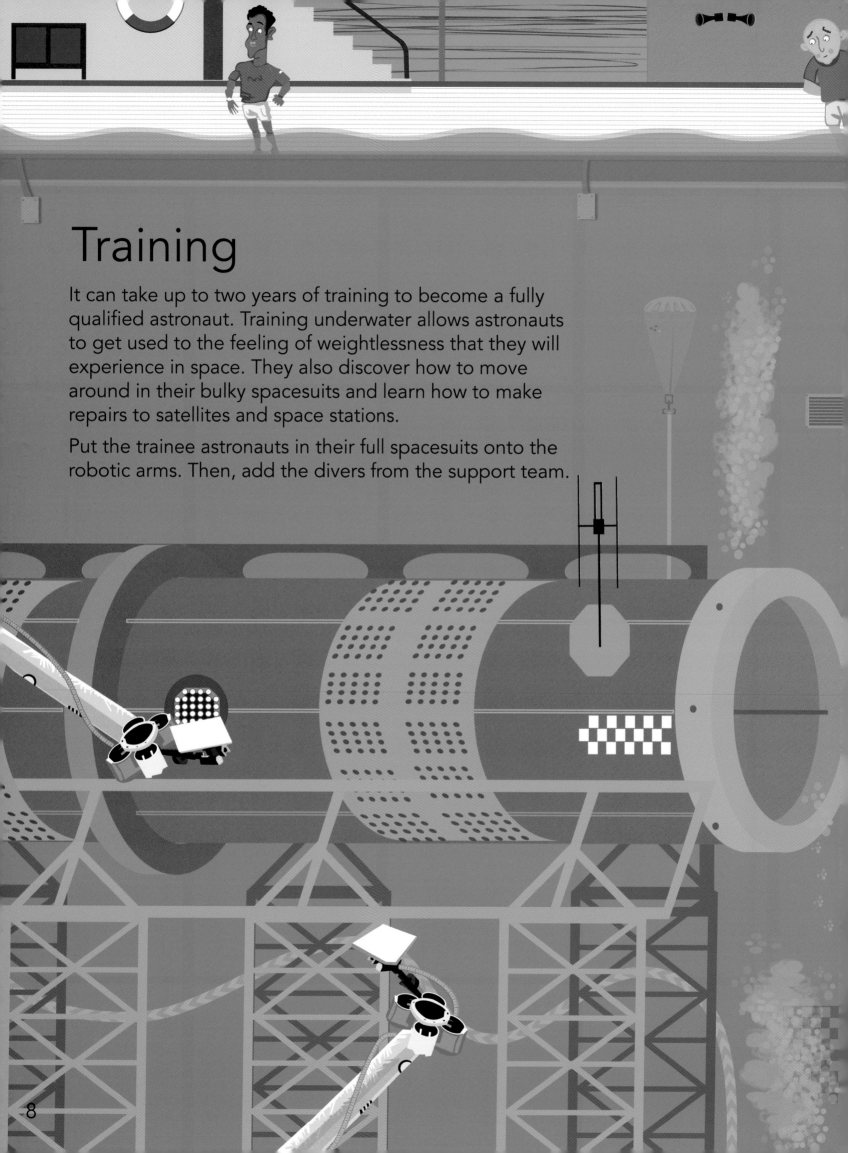

Training

It can take up to two years of training to become a fully qualified astronaut. Training underwater allows astronauts to get used to the feeling of weightlessness that they will experience in space. They also discover how to move around in their bulky spacesuits and learn how to make repairs to satellites and space stations.

Put the trainee astronauts in their full spacesuits onto the robotic arms. Then, add the divers from the support team.

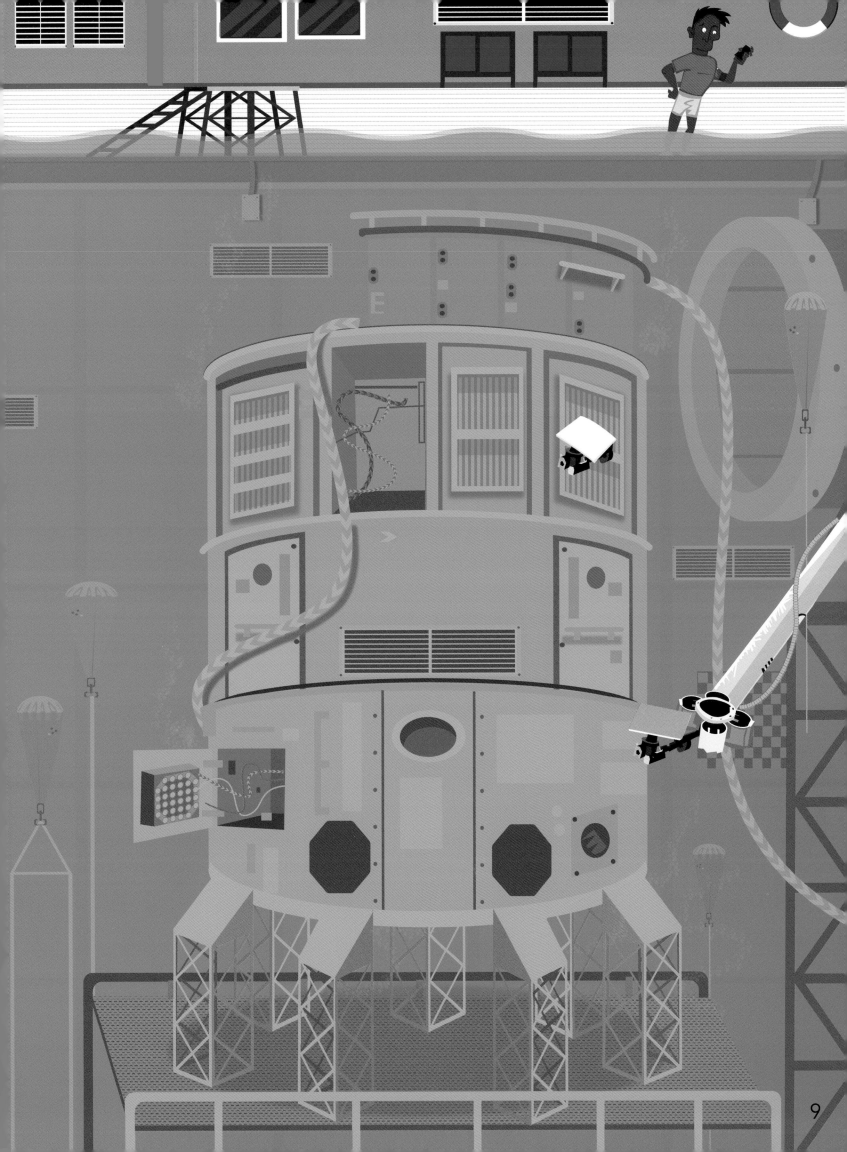

Floating in Space

These trainee astronauts are experiencing a different type of weightlessness. They're in a specially modified jet that's flying up and down like a rollercoaster ride. The jet accelerates steeply at an angle, then plunges, before soaring again. At the top of the flight, the passengers experience the feeling of weightlessness and float around the cabin.

Fill the cabin with people spinning and twirling in midair.

Before a launch

A rocket is on the launchpad, the engineers have made all their safety checks and it's time for the crew to enter the spacecraft.

Add the stickers of the Russian cosmonauts in their protective spacesuits climbing the steps. Then, add the scientists, journalists and photographer who have come to wish them well.

Liftoff!

The cosmonauts have been in the crew capsule for two and a half hours, working with the ground controllers who prepare for the rocket launch. Then, the countdown begins...
10... 9... 8... 7... 6... 5... 4... 3... 2... 1... 0. Liftoff!

Follow the labels on the sticker pages to build the rocket.

The emergency escape rocket. The crew can use it if something goes wrong during liftoff.

The nose cone containing the crew capsule is covered in a heat shield.

This part is known as the third stage. It powers the crew capsule into orbit.

The second stage of the rocket. It keeps firing after the booster rockets have used up all their fuel.

The booster rockets provide extra power during liftoff. They burn all their fuel in less than two minutes, then fall off.

The service tower that supports the rocket before the launch. It moves back at liftoff.

Mission Control

Every space flight is backed up by Mission Control. There's lots of whooping and hugging going on as this team has successfully landed an exploration rover on Mars. Its mission is to look for signs of water and life on the planet, and take photos of its surface to beam back to Earth.

Add all the scientists and controllers congratulating and high-fiving each other.

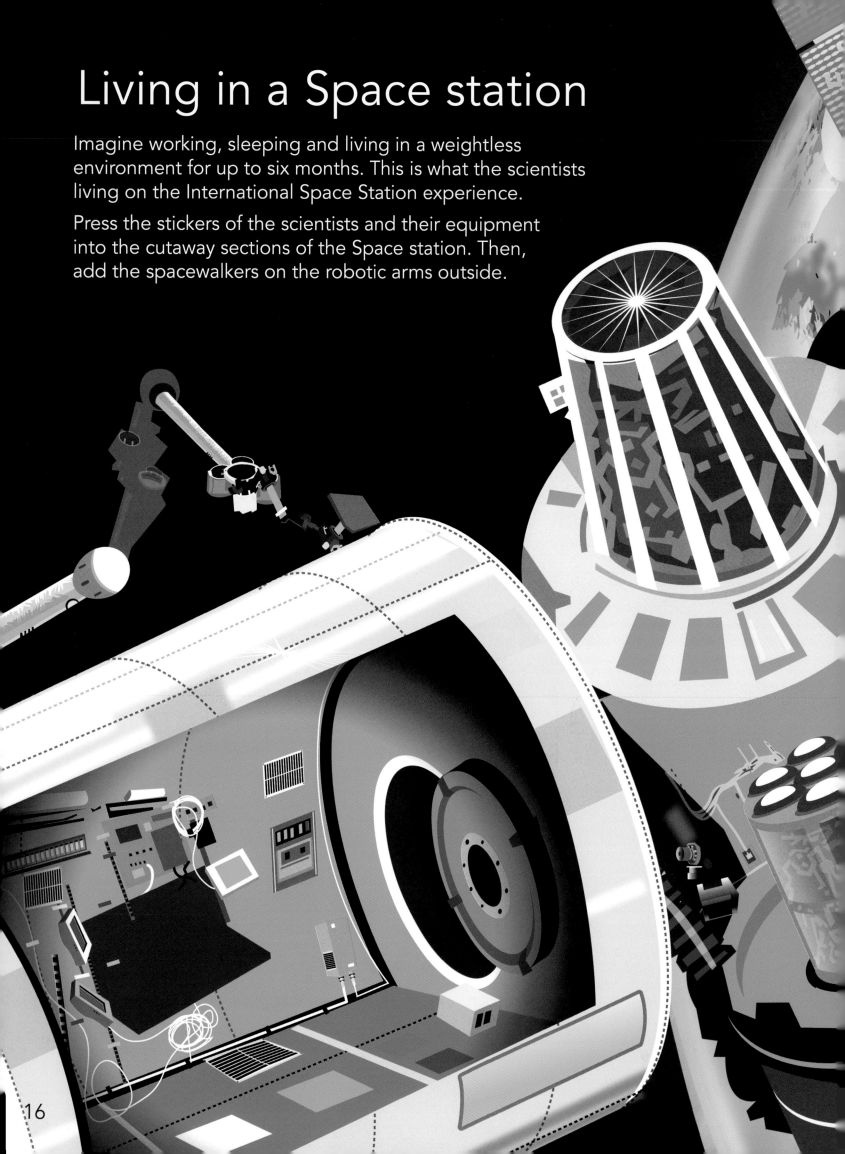

Living in a Space station

Imagine working, sleeping and living in a weightless environment for up to six months. This is what the scientists living on the International Space Station experience.

Press the stickers of the scientists and their equipment into the cutaway sections of the Space station. Then, add the spacewalkers on the robotic arms outside.

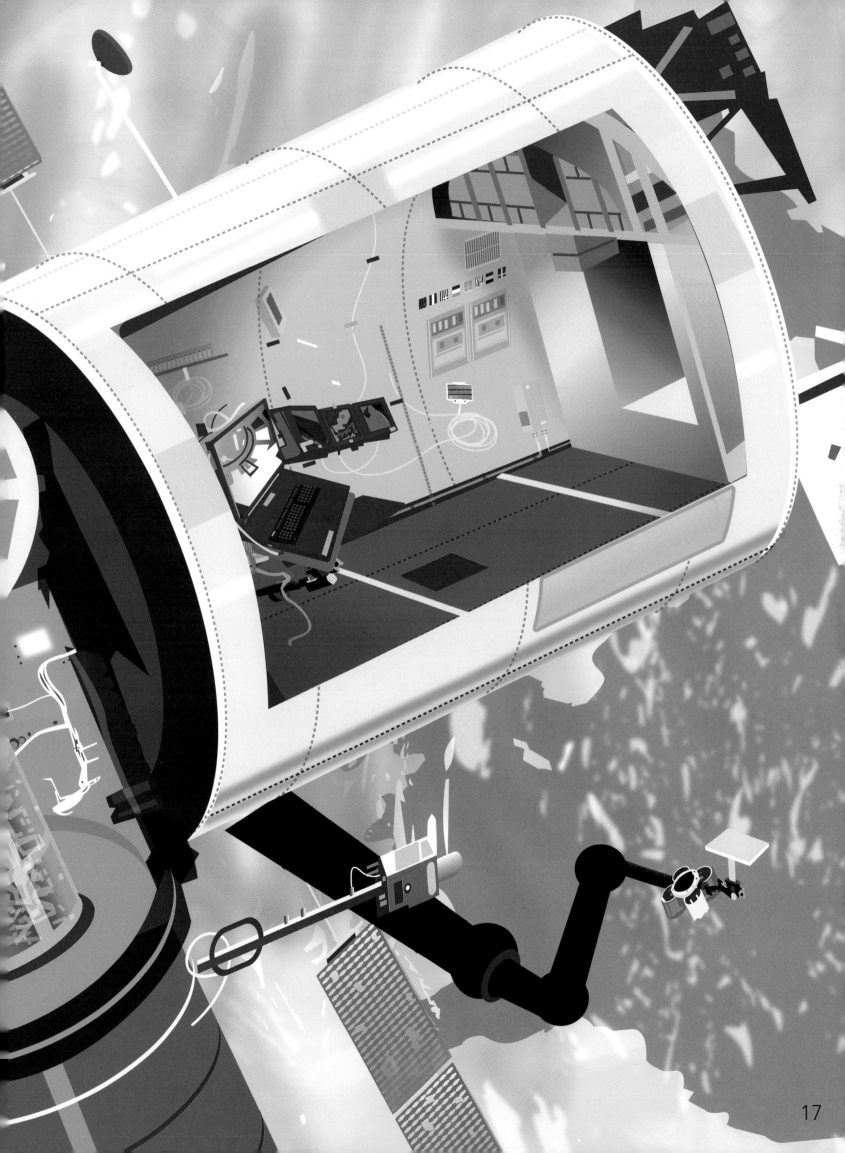

Journeys into Space

Find out some fascinating facts about the history of space flight on these two pages.

Read the facts, then press the correct sticker next to them.

First rocket to reach Space

★ 3rd October 1942

★ a missile built and launched in Germany

★ the first man-made object to go through the Earth's atmosphere and reach the edge of Space

★ designed by rocket scientist Wernher von Braun

First living creatures in Space

★ 20th February 1947

★ fruit flies were sent into Space in an American V-2 rocket to see the effects of radiation

★ they were given a supply of corn to eat on the flight

★ they were ejected from the rocket in a capsule and were recovered alive

First human in Space

★ 12th April 1961

★ Russian cosmonaut Yuri Gagarin was the first man to fly into Space

★ he orbited the Earth in 108 minutes in spacecraft Vostok 1

★ he ejected from the capsule and landed safely by parachute

First animal to orbit the Earth

★ 3rd November 1957

★ Russian Space dog Laika in spacecraft Sputnik 2

★ she is thought to have died a few hours after blast-off from overheating and stress (although at the time it was reported that she had lived for about a week)

First craft to orbit the Earth

★ 4th October 1957

★ Russian satellite Sputnik 1 circled the Earth

★ it sent radio signals to Earth from four antennas so its journey could be tracked by radio operators on the ground

★ it measured only 58cm (23in.) across

★ it took just over 96 minutes to complete each orbit

★ it fell from orbit after three months in Space and burned up on re-entering the Earth's atmosphere

First woman in Space

★ 16th June 1963

★ Russian cosmonaut Valentina Tereshkova

★ she spent three days alone in spacecraft Vostok 6, completing 49 orbits of the Earth

★ she also landed safely by parachute after ejecting from the capsule

Space Shuttle Columbia

★ American Space Shuttle launched 12th April 1981

★ blasted off like a rocket, but landed like a plane on a runway

★ launched on 28 missions

First men on the Moon

★ 20th July 1969

★ American astronauts Neil Armstrong and Buzz Aldrin on the Apollo 11 mission

★ they landed in a lunar module called The Eagle

★ they spent 21 hours on the Moon, including two and a half outside the lunar module

★ collected samples of Moon rock, took photographs and performed different scientific experiments

First Space station

★ Russian Space station Salyut 1 launched on 19th April 1971

★ crews flew to it in Soyuz spacecraft

★ the first crew had to abort their mission when the docking hatch failed

★ after 175 days in Space, it burned up as it re-entered the Earth's atmosphere

Is there anybody out there?

For as long as people have studied the stars and planets, they have wondered whether there are other things living in space. Who knows? There may be a world far, far away in the galaxy that could support alien life.

Fill this spaceship with alien stickers.

Moon base

Will it be possible for people to live on the Moon? It could happen one day, but can you imagine drinking water that has been created chemically, constantly breathing recycled air and growing everything you eat?

Fill this imaginary Moon base with stickers.

Tourists of the future

Bing... bong... "Good afternoon ladies and gentlemen. Flight 278X to Space is now ready for boarding."

Put the stickers of the passengers and spectators in the observation tower, then add the spacecraft around the terminal building.

This edition first published in 2016 by Usborne Publishing Ltd., Usborne House, 83-85 Saffron Hill, London, England. www.usborne.com Copyright © 2016, 2015 Usborne Publishing Ltd. The name Usborne and the devices ♀ ⊕ are Trade Marks of Usborne Publishing Ltd. This edition first published in America in 2016. U.E.